Say It... Or Not?

Workbook

Happy Frog Press

First Printing, 2017
ISBN 978-0-9953208-5-7
Happy Frog Press
www.HappyFrogPress.com

Introduction

Welcome to the "Say It... Or Not?" workbook! Inside you'll find 54 pages of worksheets that help children with ASD/ADHD understand and practice what to say... and what not to say... in real-life social situations.

Filtering thoughts can be a challenge for these kids. Our worksheets help them find appropriate words for over fifty challenging social situations.

In the following pages, your learner will begin by thinking about how people feel if you say something nice versus something rude or awkward.

Next, they'll evaluate specific examples to decide whether it is okay to say, or not. Finally, given a specific scenario, learners will decide what is a good thing to say in that situation.

Students begin with multiple choice answers, but progress to independent thinking. The workbook also steps the learner from family-based situations, to dealing with friends and finally to community settings.

By the end of the workbook, your students will have a better understanding of how their words impact other people and will be able to make better choices. A great achievement!

Our workbooks are designed to appeal to unmotivated learners. We use a colorful design, large print and lots of white space. We wish you and your learner all the best!

Additional Resources

Students often benefit from using a variety of resources that target the same skill. The variety allows them to maintain a higher interest level and consolidate their learning.

Happy Frog has a complementary "Say It... Or Not?" app that can help your learner. The app is available for Apple and Android devices.

You can find out more about our social skills apps at www.HappyFrogApps.com

We recommend using both apps and workbooks as the apps:

- Give instant feedback.
- Include an engaging Reward Center to motivate students
- Allow independent use.
- Most of all... kids LOVE screen time. So life will be easier for you!

About Happy Frog Press

Happy Frog Apps & Happy Frog Press create high-quality resources for elementary-aged children with autism and other social/language challenges.

We believe that all children can learn – as long as we provide a learning environment that suits their needs.

www.HappyFrogApps.com

Talking with Family

Your sister asks what you think of her short story. You think it is dull and full of mistakes.

You say, "I wanted to know what would happen at the end!"

How does your sister feel about what you said?

Identify the correct answer:

Thrilled	Sad

Talking with Family

You asked your mom to record your favourite show. She forgot.

You say, "I only asked you to do one small thing. I hate you!"

How does your mom feel about what you said?

Identify the correct answer:

Pleased with your manners	Offended

Talking with Family

Your mom says you owe her ten dollars for breaking a window with the basketball. You are mad because now you can't go to the movies.

You say, "No! That's my money!"

How does your mom feel about what you said?

Identify the correct answer:

Unhappy	Proud

Talking with Family

Your grandmother has her music on and she asks if you like it. You don't like it at all.

You say, "It's interesting!"

How does your grandmother feel about what you said?

Write your answer:

Talking with Family

Your brother pushes in front of you and sits in the chair you usually sit in at dinner. You are mad at him.

You say, “Move it, idiot.”

How does your brother feel about what you said?

Write your answer:

____

____

Talking with Family

Your mom asks you to clean your room.

You tell her, "Why can't you do it?"

How does your mom feel about what you said?

Write your answer:

____

____

Talking with Family

You and your bother both want the last piece of cake. Your brother's first piece was bigger than yours.

You say, "You've already had more. I want this piece"

Is that okay to say?

Identify the correct answer:

Don't say it.	It's okay.

Talking with Family

Your mom asks if you are full. You're still hungry.

You say, "I'm still quite hungry. Is there more?"

Is that okay to say?

Identify the correct answer:

It's rude. Don't say it.

It's fine. You can say it.

Talking with Family

Your bother is watching TV but the sound is way too loud. It's giving you a headache.

You say, "Turn that thing down. It's driving me crazy!"

Is that okay to say?

Identify the correct answer:

It's rude. Don't say it.	Yes

Talking with Family

You drop your cup and break it. You look across at your baby cousin. Your Mom comes back in the room and you decide what to tell her.

You say, "Joe knocked my cup over. Babies are so clumsy"

Is that okay to say?

Write your answer:

____

____

Talking with Family

Your mom opens the door and greets your cousins who have arrived. You are in the middle of playing a computer game.

You say, "Go away!"

Is that okay to say?

Write your answer:

____

____

Talking with Family

Your mom asks for help in raking the yard.
You hate doing yard chores.

You say, “Okay.”

Is that okay to say?

Write your answer:

____

____

Talking with Family

Your mom asks who put the empty mayo bottle back in the refrigerator. It was you.

What should you say or do?

Identify the correct answer:

"It's not my fault. Dad ate most of it."

"You pick on me every time."

"I'm sorry, Mom. It was me."

Talking with Family

Your two-year-old cousin wants to blow out your birthday candles with you. You want to do it by yourself.

What should you say or do?

Identify the correct answer:

"Go away. It's MY birthday."

"No. I don't want to."

"Let's do it together and then I will have a turn by myself."

Talking with Family

Dad asks you to help with preparing dinner.

What should you say or do?

Identify the correct answer:

"Okay. What can I do?"

"I hate cooking."

"Whatever."

Talking with Family

Your brother is playing games on your phone without asking you. You have told him not to do that.

What should you say or do?

Write your answer:

____

____

Talking with Family

Your mom asks you to clean up the mess in the living room. You are mad because you didn't make the mess. Your sister did.

What should you say or do?

Write your answer:

Talking with Family

It's time for you to leave your four-year-old cousin's birthday party. You didn't really enjoy yourself because the little kids were loud and annoying.

What should you say or do?

Write your answer:

____

____

Talking with Friends

Your friend asks for the marker she lent you.
You can't find it.

You say, "You never lent me a marker."

How does your friend feel about what you said?

Identify the correct answer:

Thrilled	Angry

Talking with Friends

Your friend asks you if you like his new backpack. You don't.

You say, "It's got a cool zipper!"

How does your friend feel about what you said?

Identify the correct answer:

Disappointed

Cheerful

Talking with Friends

As you ride home from school, your friend asks if you want to come over to her house and play. You can't because you have Karate class.

You say, "Don't ask me."

How does your friend feel about what you said?

Identify the correct answer:

Irritated	Disappointed but understanding.

Talking with Friends

Your best friend asks if you think her Mom is too old to have her hair dyed pink. You think she is too old.

You say, "My mom says that you are never too old to try something new."

How does your friend feel about what you said?

Write your answer:

____

____

Talking with Friends

Your friend comes to school with a new shirt she bought with her own money. You think it is a horrible color.

You say, "That color is horrible."

How does your friend feel about what you said?

Write your answer:

____

____

Talking with Friends

Your friend asks for a sip of your soda. You don't want to catch her cold.

You say, "No way."

How does your friend feel about what you said?

Write your answer:

____

____

Talking with Friends

Your friend asks if you like her mom playing the piano. She is very good, but you don't like that kind of music.

You say, "You're joking! I hate it!"

Is that okay to say?

Identify the correct answer:

Yes	No

Talking with Friends

You watch your friend's team lose an important basketball game. Afterwards, he asks you how he played. You think he made lots of mistakes.

You say, "You made sooo many mistakes!"

Is that okay to say?

Identify the correct answer:

It's rude. Don't say it.	Yes

Talking with Friends

Your friend knocks at the door wanting to play. You don't want to play.

You say, "My mom needs me to help her. Let's play tomorrow."

Is that okay to say?

Identify the correct answer:

It's fine. You can say it.

It's rude. Don't say it.

Talking with Friends

Your friend asks if he can borrow your skateboard. You think he is too heavy for it.

You say, "Sure. Please take care with it."

Is that okay to say?

Write your answer:

____

____

Talking with Friends

Your friend comes to school with a really weird haircut. He thinks it looks great and asks what you think.

You say, "I like how you try out different hair cuts."

Is that okay to say?

Write your answer:

____

____

Talking with Friends

Your friend's mom offers you a cookie that you don't like.

You say, "Mrs. B, don't you know I don't like cookies?"

Is that okay to say?

Write your answer:

____

____

Talking with Friends

Your friend tells you that her cat died on the weekend.

What should you say or do?

Identify the correct answer:

"I'm sorry to hear that."

"I don't like animals."

"You won't have to buy cat food anymore!"

Talking with Friends

Your friend's dad starts telling you a joke that he has told you already. He asks you if he has told you this one before.

What should you say or do?

Identify the correct answer:

"You've told me about ten times! It's boring."

"Yes, and it wasn't funny the first time."

"Go ahead, Mr. G."

Talking with Friends

Your Chinese friend asks you to have dinner with his family. You can't use chopsticks and you worry that you might look silly.

What should you say or do?

Identify the correct answer:

"Can you teach me to use chopsticks?"

"Chinese food tastes awful."

"I don't want to come to your house."

Talking with Friends

Your friend has to go to bed at 7:30. She asks if you think that is too early. You do think it is early.

What should you say or do?

Write your answer:

____

____

Talking with Friends

Your play chess with your friend and lose the game. You are mad because you lost.

What should you say or do?

Write your answer:

____

____

Talking with Friends

Your laptop breaks when your friend is using it. You know it was not his fault, but you are upset.

What should you say or do?

Write your answer:

____

____

Talking in the Community

Your teacher asks if you liked the book she recommended. You found it boring.

You say, "It was so boring. I only read one page."

How does your teacher feel about what you said?

Identify the correct answer:

Appreciated

Insulted

Talking in the Community

Your friend's mom serves you no-brand-cola with dinner. You only drink Coca-Cola and hate the no-name stuff.

You say, "Thank you." And just take one small sip.

How does your friend's mom feel about what you said?

Identify the correct answer:

Pleased	Offended

Talking in the Community

Your neighbor offers you a coat which she thinks you might like. It doesn't look like it would fit and it's a horrible color.

You say, "Yuck. It's horrible."

How does your neighbor feel about what you said?

Identify the correct answer:

Taken aback with your rudeness

Happy

Talking in the Community

Your family is having dinner with your dad's boss. His wife gives you a big serving of beans. You hate beans.

You say, "Thank you."

How does your hostess feel about what you said?

Write your answer:

____

____

Talking in the Community

Your neighbor complains about the ball that you kicked into her yard.

You tell her, "It's not my fault."

How does your neighbor feel about what you said?

Write your answer:

____

____

Talking in the Community

Your new teacher wants to know if you like her class. You prefer your old teacher.

You say, “You explain things very well.”

How does your new teacher feel about what you said?

Write your answer:

____

____

Talking in the Community

Your dad's friend offers to buy you a small burger. You want a large one.

You say, "Yes, please!"

Is that okay to say?

Identify the correct answer:

It's rude. Don't say it.	Yes

Talking in the Community

You are mad at a classmate because he laughed at you yesterday. As you arrive at school, the classmate smiles at you and says, "Hi."

You say, "Go away!"

Is that okay to say?

Identify the correct answer:

Yes	It's rude. Don't say it.

Talking in the Community

Your teacher tells you to repeat your answer. She couldn't hear you.

You say, "What's wrong with you? I said FIVE."

Is that okay to say?

Identify the correct answer:

It's fine. You can say it.

It's rude. Don't say it.

Talking in the Community

Your teacher loves his new car. He asks what you think. You think the car is ugly.

You say, "It's cool."

Is that okay to say?

Write your answer:

Talking in the Community

The substitute teacher keeps calling you Peter, but your name is John.

You say, “Can’t you read? I’m John!”

Is that okay to say?

Write your answer:

____

____

Talking in the Community

The librarian asks you and your friend to be quiet. You are mad because it was your friend making the noise, not you.

You say, "Try talking to her about that."

Is that okay to say?

Write your answer:

____

____

Talking in the Community

You are at a restaurant and the hostess takes a really long time to come and greet you. She asks how you are doing.

What should you say or do?

Identify the correct answer:

"Good. We need a table for four."

"Can we just get a table already?"

"Annoyed. We had to wait a long time."

Talking in the Community

Your friend's dad asks you to pet their dog.
You are a bit scared of dogs.

What should you say or do?

Identify the correct answer:

"Dogs are dirty. I'm not touching him."

"I hate dogs."

"Can you hold his leash while I pet him?"

Talking in the Community

You stayed over at your friend's house. The bed was really uncomfortable. His mom asks how you slept.

What should you say or do?

Identify the correct answer:

"Not bad. Thank you."

"I slept terribly in that old bed."

"That bed stopped me sleeping. It's so hard."

Talking in the Community

You need to borrow scissors from your classmate because you can't find yours.

What should you say or do?

Write your answer:

____

____

Talking in the Community

The librarian tells you that you can't borrow any more books until you pay your library fine.

What should you say or do?

Write your answer:

___

___

Talking in the Community

At a restaurant, the waiter brings you spaghetti, but you ordered a hamburger.

What should you say or do?

Write your answer:

___

___

Answer Key

Page 4	*Thrilled*
Page 5	*Offended*
Page 6	*Unhappy*
Page 7	*Pleased*
Page 8	*Annoyed*
Page 9	*Frustrated*
Page10	*Don't say it.*
Page 11	*It's fine. You can say it.*
Page 12	*It's rude. Don't say it.*
Page 13	*No*
Page 14	*No*
Page 15	*Yes*
Page 16	*I'm sorry, mom. It was me.*
Page 17	*Let's do it together and then I will have a turn by myself.*
Page 28	*Okay. What can I do?*
Page 19	*Please don't use my phone without asking.*
Page 20	*I can help clean up, but it was Lisa who made the mess.*
Page 21	*I've got to go now. Thanks for inviting me.*
Page 22	*Angry*
Page 23	*Cheerful*
Page 24	*Irritated*
Page 25	*Relieved*
Page 26	*Embarrassed and upset*
Page 27	*Upset*
Page 28	*Embarrassed and upset*

Answer Key continued...

Page 29	*It's rude. Don't say it.*
Page 30	*It's fine. You can say it.*
Page 31	*Yes*
Page 32	*Yes*
Page 33	*No*
Page 34	*I'm sorry to hear that.*
Page 35	*Go ahead, Mr G.*
Page 36	*Can you teach me how to use chopsticks?*
Page 37	*Maybe you can discuss it with your parents?*
Page 38	*Congratulations. Thanks for playing.*
Page 39	*Don't worry. It's not your fault.*
Page 40	*Insulted*
Page 41	*Pleased*
Page 42	*Taken aback with your rudeness*
Page 43	*Pleased with your manners*
Page 44	*Annoyed that you are not taking responsibility*
Page 45	*Pleased*
Page 46	*Yes*
Page 47	*It's rude. Don't say it.*
Page 48	*It's rude. Don't say it.*
Page 49	*Yes*
Page 50	*No*
Page 51	*No*
Page 52	*Good. We need a table for four.*
Page 53	*Can you hold his leash while I pet him?*
Page 54	*Not bad. Thank you.*
Page 55	*May I borrow your scissors?*
Page 56	*How much do I owe?*
Page 57	*Excuse me. I ordered a hamburger.*